géraldine kosiak

i'm afraid

translated by alexandra childs

stewart, tabori & chang
new york

Thanks to Fabio,
Laurent Masoero, and Corinne Leneun

If one listens hard to thunder
One can hear a thousand
Different noises.

Shiki

this book belongs to:

_____

_____

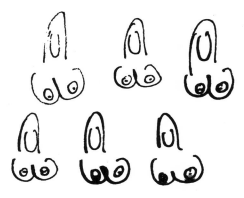

1 · I'm afraid of all those women
in magazines

**2 · I'm afraid of television,
but I still watch it**

3 · I'm afraid of men with mustaches

4 · I'm afraid of a blank page

5 · I'm afraid of all the people
I don't know

6 · I'm afraid, so I go home

7 · I'm afraid of eternal moments

8 · I'm afraid of severe depression

9 · I'm afraid of acid rain

10 · I'm afraid of being pregnant

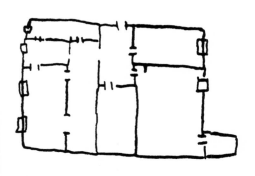

11 · I'm afraid that my rent will increase and
that I won't be able to pay it

12 · I'm afraid of people with eyeglasses

13 · I'm afraid of pollution

14 · I'm afraid that before long I'll be
nothing more than a disease

15 · I'm afraid of being afraid

16 · I'm afraid of my car breaking down

17 · I'm afraid of nuclear power

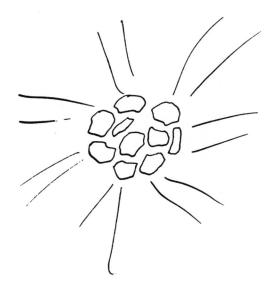

18 · I'm afraid of the end of the world

19 · I'm afraid of the buzz of blue flies

BLOOD SAUSAGE - DISAPPEAR

MORNING - BYTE - RICH - CLOSED

CANCER - PANASONIC - LASER

20 · I'm afraid of certain words

21 · I'm afraid of needles

22 · I'm afraid of red ants

**23 · I'm afraid of getting out of bed
to start the day**

24 · I'm afraid of messing up

25 · I'm afraid of snakes

26 - I'm afraid of certain stripes

27 · I'm afraid of the ruthlessly ambitious

28 · I'm afraid today of tomorrow

29 · I'm afraid of success

30 · I'm afraid of failure

31 · I'm afraid of being bored at
a dinner party

32 · I'm afraid when driving,
especially of others

33 · I'm afraid of lightning

34 · I'm afraid of real-estate agents

35 · I'm afraid of emptiness

36 · I'm afraid of people who don't look
at me when they are talking to me

37 · I'm afraid that one day there
will be no water

38 · I'm afraid of the name of this novel:
*Should We Kill Little Boys Who Put Their
Hands on Their Hips?*

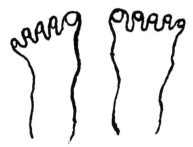

39 · I'm afraid of being cold, especially in my feet

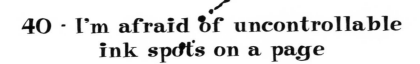

40 · I'm afraid of uncontrollable ink spots on a page

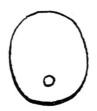

41 · I'm afraid of egotism

42 · I'm afraid of my hysterical side

43 · I'm afraid of parachuting

44 · I'm afraid of liars

45 · I'm afraid of people who abandon their dogs

46 · I'm afraid of history repeating itself

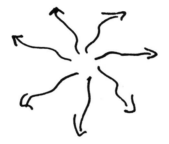

47 · I'm afraid of things being scattered

48 · I'm afraid of not being good at anything

49 · I'm afraid of losing my
hair and my teeth

50 · I'm afraid of forgetting my keys

51 · I'm afraid of ceremonies

52 · I'm afraid of thieves

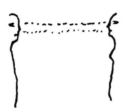

53 · I'm afraid of bad vibes

A + B = C

54 · I'm afraid of mathematics

$$A + B = C$$

55 · I'm afraid of repeating myself

56 · I'm afraid of certain noises

57 · I'm afraid of blood

58 · I'm afraid of monsters

59 · I'm afraid of never seeing
my family again

60 · I'm afraid of growing old

61 · I'm afraid of having my varicose veins removed

WHAT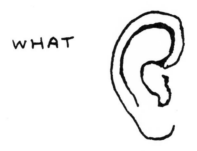

62 · I'm afraid of becoming deaf

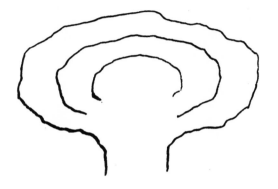

63 · I'm afraid of war

summer | autumn
spring | winter

64 · I'm afraid of the change of seasons

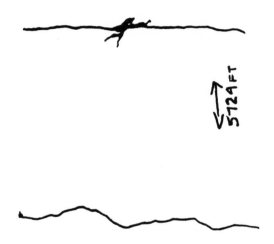

5724 FT

65 · I'm afraid of swimming in open water

66 · I'm afraid that my mail will get lost

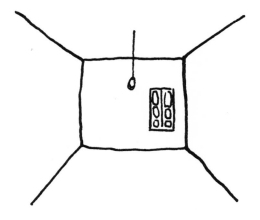

67 · I'm afraid of process servers

**68 · I'm afraid of soccer matches
that turn out badly**

69 · I'm afraid of the Ku Klux Klan

**70 · I'm afraid of hunters
(but not my father, my brother,
my grandfather, my uncle...)**

**71 · I'm afraid of rollercoasters
at amusement parks**

72 · I'm afraid of mystics

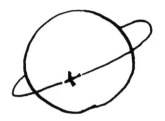

73 · I'm afraid of not having enough time to visit all the countries in the world

**74 · I'm afraid of rotting underground
and stinking**

75 · I'm afraid of not reaching the moon

**76 · I'm afraid of choosing the
wrong religion**

77 · I'm afraid of racists

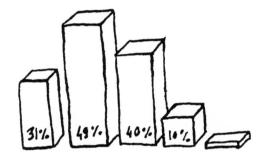

78 · I'm afraid of politicians who create their own policies

79 · I'm afraid of losing time

80 · I'm afraid of not being funny

bla bla bla bla
bla bla bla bla bla

81 · I'm afraid of certain explanations

82 · I'm afraid of making spelling mistakes

83 · I'm afraid of choking

84 · I'm afraid of being paralyzed

85 · I'm afraid of habits

GERALDINE
KOSIAK

86 · I'm afraid that people will forget me

First published in France under the title *J'ai Peur* © Editions du Seuil, 1995.

Translated by Alexandra M. Childs.

Published in 1997 and distributed in the U.S. by Stewart, Tabori & Chang, a division of U.S. Media Holdings, Inc.
115 West 18th Street, New York, NY 10011

Distributed in Canada by General Publishing Company Ltd.
30 Lesmill Road, Don Mills, Ontario, M3B 2T6, Canada

Distributed in Australia by Peribo Pty Ltd.
58 Beaumont Road, Mount Kuring-gai, NSW 2080, Australia

Distributed in all other territories by Grantham Book Services Ltd.
Isaac Newton Way, Alma Park Industrial Estate
Grantham, Lincolnshire, NG31 9SD, England

Library of Congress Cataloging-in-Publication Data

Kosiak, Géraldiné, 1969–
[J'ai peur. English]
I'm afraid/ Geraldine Kosiak
p. cm.
ISBN 1-55670-622-7 (hardcover)
1. Fear. 2. Phobias. 3. Anxiety. I. Title.
BF575.F2K67513   1997
152.4'6—dc21

97-12502

Printed in the United States of America
10 9 8 7 6 5 4 3 2 1